KERR, JAMES
BRITISH ISSUES: SPORTING
SUCCESS.

DATE DUE 796.094

GAYLORD		PRINTED IN U.S.A.

BRITISH ISSUES

SPORTING SUCCESS

James Kerr

FRANKLIN WATTS

LONDON·SYDNEY

First published in 2007 by Franklin Watts
338 Euston Road, London NW1 3BH

Franklin Watts Australia
Level 17/207 Kent Street
Sydney NSW 2000

Editor: Julia Bird
Designer: Thomas Keenes
Picture researcher: Sarah Smithies

Picture credits:
Cover: Art Seitz, ZUMA, Corbis Andrew
Wallace, Reuters, Corbis: 22. Ashley Cooper,
Corbis: 13 (b). Axel, ZUMA: 4. Bettmann,
Corbis: 7. Fabrice Coffrini, epa, Corbis: 25.
Gerry Penny, epa, Corbis: 9. Getty Images: 17.
Gideon Mendel, Corbis: 21. Jason Hawkes,
Corbis: 5. Jean-Luc Lamaere, AFP, Getty
Images: 29. Jeff Morgan sport, Alamy: 27.
London 2012 Olympic Games: 13 (t). Mark
Thompson, Getty Images: 10. Peter Andrews,
Corbis: 23. Phil Cole, Getty Images: 18.
plainpicture GmbH & Co. KG, Alamy: 20.
Popperfoto, Alamy: 4. Reuters, Corbis: 19. Rex
Features: 16. Stephen Hird, Reuters, Corbis:
Imprint page, 28. Tim Graham Picture Library,
Tim Graham via pool, Corbis: 24

Every attempt has been made to clear
copyright. Should there be any
inadvertent omission please
apply to the Publishers for rectification.

A CIP catalogue record for this book
is available from the British Library

ISBN: 978 0 7496 7603 2

Dewey Classification: 796'.0941

Printed in China

Franklin Watts is a division of
Hachette Children's Books,
an Hachette Livre UK company.

CONTENTS

2012

Many people in Britain can remember where they were and what they were doing on 6 July 2005, the day that London was named as host city for the 2012 Olympic Games.

Winning the Olympic bid

The Olympics is the world's biggest sporting event. By awarding the games to a city, the International Olympic Committee (IOC) is recognising many positive aspects of the host nation. Its facilities, its attitude to sport, even

▼ Thousands of people crowd into Trafalgar Square as London is chosen to be the host city for the 2012 Olympic Games.

the hospitality that its people are likely to show to visiting competitors and spectators are all factors that are considered. Hosting the Olympics is a matter of great national pride.

Feel good

Sport is hugely popular in Britain. In the weeks following the announcement there was great hope that London would be a successful Olympic host city, and expectations soared that British athletes would perform well on 'home soil'.

In recent times, discussions about sport in Britain have tended to focus on its problems. Participation levels, that is the number of people who are playing sport, have fallen. The general standard of facilities has also been a concern. A lack of success by many British teams on the field has added to a sense of gloom. The 'feel-good factor' that the successful bid created in many British people seemed to change this.

That sinking feeling

Since the success of London's Olympic bid, the gloom about British sport has returned. The cost of staging the Olympics is a hot topic. It is likely to be much greater than first thought. Many people are concerned about where the extra funding will come from. There are also worries about the safety of hosting the games in London, in view of the possible threat of terrorist attacks.

Will the performance of British athletes justify the huge amount of money that will need to be spent on the games?

▲ Work is already well underway in the area of East London that will be used as the site for many Olympic venues.

Will hosting the event be a positive step, helping to sow the seeds of future success in British sports at all levels?

Showcase and grass roots

Supporters of the 2012 Olympics say that the event will inspire more people to play sport in Britain. Their opponents argue that the money would be better spent on basic, grass-roots facilities that encourage sports participation all around the country, therefore improving overall levels of health and fitness.

All of these issues are under discussion, particularly in the British media. Some people may not be feeling quite so positive about 2012 now as they were in July 2005.

A RICH HISTORY

Britain has invented more major sports than any other country. Football, tennis, golf, rugby, cricket, boxing and squash are just a few of the games that were first enjoyed in England, Scotland, Wales and Ireland. Most of the rules that govern these sports were drawn up in Britain in the 19th and early 20th centuries.

Global game

Traditional British football games of the 19th century turned into the organised sport originally known as 'Association Football', the rules of which were first set down in 1863. Such is the popularity of football across the globe that it is now called 'the world game'.

However, Britain itself has enjoyed only one success in football's World Cup, and that was as long ago as 1966, when England lifted the famous trophy. Historically, England, Scotland, Wales and Northern Ireland are known as football's home nations. Of these four, only England qualified for the 2006 World Cup finals, and the team went on to perform relatively poorly at the tournament.

JUST THE FACTS

London hosted the Summer Olympics in 1908 and 1948. In 2004, Great Britain finished tenth in the Olympic medal table. After a long slump, this was regarded as a great success, and was celebrated with a victory parade through London. However, the team had come fourth out of the five largest Western European countries in the competition.

Kicked into touch

Like football, both rugby league and rugby union developed from British ball games. In Wales, rugby union is the most popular national sport. Welsh teams of the 1970s were some of the greatest to ever play the game. However, apart from winning the Six Nations Rugby Tournament in 2005, Wales has enjoyed few successes since that decade. A fine England team won the Rugby World Cup in 2003 but have faltered since. In 2006 the England team lost seven games in a row, equalling the poorest run in its history.

Out to grass

The modern game of golf was developed in Scotland. In the early 20th century, most of the world's leading golfers were British. Today, although European golfers have enjoyed great success

► England captain Bobby Moore kisses the Jules Rimet trophy following the team's World Cup victory. No British team has progressed beyond the semi-finals since 1966.

against American Ryder Cup teams, Britain has no golfing superstars.

Tennis is yet another sport that originated in Britain. In June of each year, fans watch the world's leading players compete at the home of grass-court tennis, Wimbledon. However, no British man has won the Wimbledon Championships since 1936 and the last British female champion won the tournament in 1977.

GOVERNING BODIES

Sports organisation in Britain is complex. The government department responsible for sport is the Department of Culture, Media and Sport (DCMS). Its two main aims are to encourage more sport for everyone and to re-establish Britain as a 'sporting powerhouse'.

Political issue

The government Minister for Sport reports to the Secretary of State for the DCMS. In the past, the Minister for Sport has not been a prominent position. Some argue that this shows that politicians do not think that sport is a very important issue. They say that politicians are keen to be photographed with British champions, but do not make sport a priority on the political agenda.

UK Sport

The organisation that manages sport in Britain is called UK Sport. It is responsible for encouraging participation in sport in Britain, as well as developing sports facilities. It also oversees and supplies funding for some major sporting events and supports Britain-wide sports programmes, such as the National Anti-Doping Policy which works to keep British sports drug-free. But its main focus is to ensure that the top British sportsmen and women are given the support they need to compete and be successful at an international level.

In order to carry this out, UK Sport is given a large sum of money by the government each year, which includes millions of pounds of lottery funding. The people who work for UK Sport decide how this money is spent. The organisation is therefore partly responsible for the success or failure of British competitors.

Nationwide

There are four sports councils; one for each of the four home nations. These provide a link between UK Sport and the many sports organisations at national and local level. The sports councils have to follow the aims and objectives of UK Sport in their particular region. They are given part of the money awarded to UK Sport in order to do this.

uk sport
world class success

◀ The logo of UK Sport spells out its goal of world class success for Britain.

Up for discussion

Britain is represented at the Olympic Games by the team of Great Britain. However, when the same sports feature in the Commonwealth Games, each of the home nations sends an individual team.

In tennis's international Davis Cup competition, the British team has enjoyed few successes in recent years. This used to be the case in golf's Ryder Cup. However, since the British team was replaced by a European team in 1979, Europe has won the trophy outright seven times out of a possible 14. Europe has beaten the USA in the last three competitions.

Are the number of different teams that represent the home nations in sport holding British athletes back?

Would Britain enjoy more sporting success if, as in the case of golf, Britain's best athletes or sportsmen and women were selected to join an European team?

Do British sports fans feel the same amount of pride when a team from Great Britain is successful compared with a team from, for example, Scotland?

▼ The European Ryder Cup team celebrate victory in the 2006 competition.

FUNDING

A large part of the money that funds elite sport in Britain is raised by professional clubs and the governing bodies of individual sports, for example the England and Wales Cricket Board (ECB) or Rugby Football Union (RFU).

Club revenue

All sports clubs, whether football, cricket, rugby or basketball, are run along similar lines. They raise money through ticket sales and by the sale of television rights. Money is also generated through the sale of club merchandise, such as club shirts. Sponsorship deals, in which a company can pay to have a sports stadium or in the case of Formula One motor racing, a whole team named after it, are also ways of generating money.

Most of this money is used to pay players and coaching staff, improve spectator facilities, provide training facilities, and to buy or develop new talent.

Megabucks

The money generated commercially is concentrated in just a few sports. Television companies pay money to sport governing bodies or directly to the clubs. In return, they are allowed to broadcast live matches and put together highlight shows. The Premiership football clubs have a

▼ Jenson Button celebrates his first ever Formula One motor racing victory and gives his team sponsors some television coverage.

combined turnover of over £1 billion each season, and British professional football's annual income is in the region of £2 billion. Television coverage brings in an estimated £900 million of this total. Other major sports, while nowhere near as wealthy as football, have a turnover in tens of millions. Cricket is mainly funded through a television contract, which is worth £55 million a year to the ECB over the 2006-09 seasons. Other sports benefit from special financial arrangements. British tennis is partly supported by the Wimbledon Championships, while horse-racing benefits from a betting tax.

Public support

Athletics and a number of other sports depend on public funding. UK Sport (see page 8) decides how government funding and money from the National Lottery is shared out. The national councils are responsible for distributing money to support grass-roots and community sport.

CASE STUDY
Going for gold

UK Sport will receive more than £200 million to fund all Olympic and Paralympic sports up to 2012. The 'No Compromise' plan will direct money to athletes capable of medal-winning performances. Individual sports are given funding based on a combination of past performance and future potential. Cycling and sailing look set to benefit from this decision, while those that have been less successful will be penalised. UK Sport says it can now start to work towards the 'ultimate goal' – fourth place in the 2012 Olympic medal table and first in the Paralympic medal table. To finish among the traditional Olympic power-houses of USA, China, Russia and Australia would be a great achievement for Britain, but will require a lot of work. To put it in context, in the 2004 Olympics, Britain finished tenth overall in the final medal table (see below).

▼ The medal table from the 2004 Olympic Games. Britain finished with a total of 30 medals, but this was a big improvement. In the 1996 Games, Britain won just 15 medals.

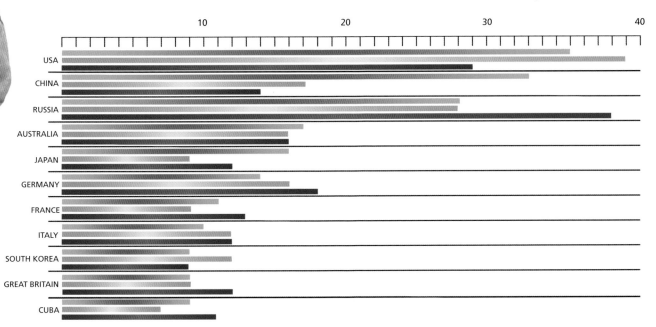

FACILITIES

In the early 20th century Britain had some of the largest sports grounds in the world. However, the level of comfort and facilities they offered would be considered totally unacceptable by modern standards.

Change for good

For many years, the overall standard of sports facilities in Britain dropped compared with other more economically developed countries (MEDCs). Two tragic events occurred in the 1980s to change this. In 1985, 52 supporters died during a fire at the football stadium in Bradford. In 1989, 96 fans were crushed to death in an overcrowded Hillsborough during an FA Cup tie. These events helped initiate sweeping reforms to British sport facilities.

Overall standards have improved and football stadia are now all-seater. World-class sporting events are hosted at the Millennium Stadium in Cardiff and Wembley Stadium in London. The improvement is set to continue as work progresses on the 2012 Olympic facilities.

Water shortage

At recreational level, the standard of facilities is not so strong. For example, there were only 13 Olympic

CASE STUDY
Selling out

- During the 1980s, large amounts of land that had been used for public recreation were sold by local authorities. The developers who bought these playing fields used them to build private housing. Many people argued that this was damaging to sport in Britain.

- UK Sport says that it will protect playing fields. But in June 2006 the Minister for Sport, Richard Caborn, reported that in England nearly 34,000

sports pitches have disappeared over the last 13 years. According to The National Playing Fields Association (NPFA) an average of one playing field every day is still under threat from building development.

- In Scotland, campaigners have praised the efforts of sportscotland (Scotland's national agency for sport) to protect sporting facilities. But because sportscotland can only object to plans that involve the loss of land of 0.4

hectares (around 4000 sq metres) or more, smaller facilities such as tennis courts and bowling greens, as well as larger green spaces in towns and cities, can be built on without protection. A spokesman for NPFA Scotland says: 'We are aware of substantial losses of tennis courts and five-a-side pitches over recent years, but these losses don't appear in any statistics.'

▶ The NPFA believes that many playing areas are under threat in Britain.

JUST THE FACTS

The rebuilt 90,000-seat Wembley Stadium finally opened its doors in May 2007. Years of delay and rising costs meant that the stadium's budget spiralled from an original £458 million to over £800 million. More than £160 million of public money was spent on the new stadium.

◀ Wembley Stadium is just one new venue for the 2012 Olympics.

size (50 metre) swimming pools in Britain in 2005. This compares badly with other MEDCs. A visitor to an Australian town or city cannot help but notice the number of excellent swimming facilities. Many people would argue that there is a direct link between the number and quality of these facilities and Australia's ongoing success in international swimming competitions.

SPORT AND SOCIETY

In the days when many sports were amateur, the gap between recreational players and those who played for the top teams was not so great. In the past, sportsmen and women who represented Britain at international level would return to their day jobs after the game.

Superstars

It is hard to imagine today's sporting stars competing on an amateur level. In most sports, training, playing, touring and, for the top players, marketing and press commitments, are a full-time job. Some sports stars enjoy multi-millionaire status. Top cricketers can expect to earn up to

£300,000 per year. Meanwhile, a football player for a top club in the Premiership can command a wage of over £100,000 per week. In golf and tennis, British players compete for large sums of prize money. Singles champions in the US Open tennis championship now receive over $1 million (around £500,000) in prize money. Even in sports that remain amateur, there is money available in the form of grants such as UK Sport's Talented Athlete Scholarship Scheme (TASS).

Played out

The gap between elite and recreational sport has grown wider. It seems that the gap between interest in sport and participation is also increasing. Sport is hugely popular in Britain, but it is worrying that many people prefer to watch the stars on television than take part themselves.

There are all sorts of issues at stake here. For young people, sport is in competition with many more alternative amusements. In the past, playing football would have meant a Sunday afternoon kick around in the park. But it is now possible to play football matches on games consoles at any time. The level of televised sport has also greatly increased in the past 20 years, particularly with the introduction of sports channels on satellite television.

Couch potatoes

Most experts would agree that there is a direct link between levels of sports participation and physical fitness. Recent reports on health statistics in Britain highlight the decline in physical fitness. Most worrying are levels of obesity, which have rocketed to become some of the worst in Europe.

◀ As recently as 1995, when this photo of England and Wales playing in the Five Nations Championship was taken, rugby was still an amateur sport.

▼ A recent survey of Britain's most popular sports showed the difference in the number of people watching the sport (left) and taking part themselves (right).

Football		Tennis		Athletics		Snooker		Cricket		Golf	
46%	10%	18%	3%	18%	2%	17%	5%	17%	2%	11%	6%

THE BUSINESS OF SPORT

Football, cricket, rugby union, rugby league, tennis and golf have always been popular as recreational and spectator sports in Britain. Today, the organisations that run these sports and the top clubs make huge amounts of money from ticket sales, merchandising and sponsorship.

Buy out

In other countries sports clubs are often owned by the fans, for example many of the leading Spanish football clubs, including Barcelona. This is rarely the case in Britain. Recently, leading sports clubs have been bought by wealthy business people from overseas. Some critics believe that these new owners are more interested in making money from the clubs than in pleasing the fans.

Dominance of the big sports

Football, rugby, cricket and golf have traditionally been the most popular games in Britain. But some of the money that they generate is put back into marketing, ensuring that they continue to have a high profile in British sport. Critics say that it is very difficult for other lower profile sports to get a look-in.

◀ The Russian billionaire owner of Chelsea Football Club, Roman Abramovich.

The football monster

Each year, the football season seems to start earlier. The level of coverage that football now receives partly reflects the extended length of the football season. There was once a time when it was possible to play both professional football and cricket. Famous players who excelled in both sports include Denis Compton (Arsenal and Middlesex) and Ian Botham (Scunthorpe and Somerset). But the traditional winter and summer split that allowed them to play both sports no longer exists.

Some of the leading Premiership clubs are businesses, listed on the Stock Exchange. As well as achieving success on the pitch, they must make money for the

Up for discussion

Overseas players joined British sports teams in increasing numbers from the late 1970s onwards. Some commentators argue that the presence of foreign stars allows home-grown players to test their skills against the best week-in and week-out. Others say that foreign players reduce opportunities for talented youngsters from Britain to compete at the highest level.

Cricket is one of the sports to limit the number of overseas players per team. Should football and other sports follow cricket's example?

▼ County cricket teams balance both local and overseas players.

people who own the clubs – the shareholders. It is in the interest of the clubs to organise as many fixtures as they can, because this increases gate money and television revenue. But is this at the expense of the performance of the home nation teams in major tournaments?

Before recent tournaments, some fans, journalists and even coaches have questioned the national teams' prospects. They claim that players are turning up having barely stopped playing league football. The long Premiership season, unlike many leagues in Europe, has no mid-winter break. There has been speculation that players have arrived at training camps worn out or not fully fit. This has been enhanced by the trend of clubs playing exhibition matches overseas in a bid to attract new fans and thereby increase revenue.

The money game

Lack of success breeds lack of success. Money is now key to maintaining high standards in the top sports. Once a team does badly, ticket sales go down. Even within football, the rich clubs receive most of the television revenue while clubs in the lower divisions struggle to survive.

SUCCESS STORIES

There is one area of sport that was developed in Britain and in which British athletes have continued to be successful. This is the range of sports dedicated to athletes with disabilities.

The Paralympics

In 1948, a sports tournament was held at the Stoke Mandeville hospital in England for World War II servicemen who were recovering from spinal injuries. In 1960, athletes with physical disabilities competed in Rome, following the end of the Olympic Games. This was the first Paralympics, which is now held every four years in the same city as the Olympics.

The highest level

The Paralympics involves athletes from six different disability groups, but focuses on the athletes' performance at elite level rather than their disability. In 1960, 400 athletes representing 23 countries competed in the world's first Paralympics.

▶ Britain's most successful Paralympian of all time, Tanni Grey-Thompson, in action at the Paralympics in Athens, 2004.

In Athens in 2004, 2806 athletes representing 136 nations were involved. Events from the games were broadcast on television in 25 countries.

Great British champions

The British team has never finished outside the top five of the Paralympic medal table, and has been second several times, including the games in 2000 and 2004, when 35 gold medals were won. The great wheelchair racer Tanni Grey-Thompson won her 11th gold medal and was competing in her fifth successive games. A crop of rising stars also did well, particularly in the swimming and cycling competitions.

Other successes

There are many other sports in which the British compete with some success. In recent years, Britain has excelled in cycling, judo, sailing, rowing, equestrian events, darts, snooker and badminton. However, many of these sports do not receive a great deal of newspaper and television coverage, except during major tournaments.

Beth Tweddle, the first British World Champion gymnast, came third in the 2006 BBC Sports Personality of the Year competition. In a recent interview however, she described how she is barely recognised in her home city of Liverpool.

CASE STUDY
Olympic hero

- If Beth Tweddle needed inspiration, she need look no further than Britain's Steve Redgrave. In 1984, Steve competed in his first Olympic Games, winning a gold medal in the coxed four rowing competition. In 2000, he competed in his fifth and final Olympics, where he won a fifth rowing gold medal. This achievement has never been matched by any other Olympic rower.

- Supreme sporting success has made Britain's greatest ever Olympian a famous character. Steve Redgrave received a knighthood in 2001. He uses this fame to inspire others, and his charitable trust has already earned over £5 million. This money is directed towards activities and facilities that improve the lives of young people. The latest project, providing rowing machines for inner city schools, may help a future British Olympian row to the gold medal.

▼ Steve Redgrave is presented with his fifth Olympic rowing gold medal by Princess Anne in 2000.

SPORT AND EDUCATION

A great deal of attention has been paid to the health of the British population in recent years. Bad diets and a lack of physical activity are combining to create a health crisis. A 2001 report showed that if obesity continues to rise at the current rate, more than one in four adults will be obese by 2010.

Out of shape

There is particular concern about the level of obesity among young people. The community sport council, Sport England, reports that one in ten children are clinically obese, increasing their risk of heart attacks, diabetes, arthritis, bronchitis and other serious illnesses. Sports activity has also fallen, particularly in the 16–24 age group. Experts have pointed to a number of reasons for this. The popularity of home entertainment is one. In 2005, the National Children's Bureau reported that a lack of outside play areas and the fear that the outdoor world is unsafe also lead parents to keep children indoors.

The fitness factor

In recent years, education decision-makers have looked at the way in which PE might be used to tackle obesity. Sport at school is compulsory for all students up to the age of 16. But

◄ Sport is a great way to stay healthy but some young people in Britain take part in less than one hour of physical exercise per week.

the amount of time devoted to it is small. By ensuring one hour of games per week for all pupils, regardless of ability, it is hoped that overall fitness levels in young people will improve.

Aiming higher

The latest inspections of PE in secondary schools reported improved standards of teaching and performance. But the inspections went on to say that in a quarter of schools teaching PE is severely restricted because of poor facilities. Of particular concern were outdoor play areas. In some schools, ground surfaces were disintegrating. The inspections also highlighted a lack of sporting equipment. The report concluded that conditions must be improved if young people are to achieve high standards in school sport.

Up for discussion

During the 1980s, many schools banned competitive sports. This was a result of concerns about games in which there were winners and losers. The situation has now changed in most schools, and PE again involves some competition. Teachers are careful to match pupils according to their ability.

Some believe that the only way to produce top-class athletes is to focus on the teaching of skills in conditions of competitive pressure. Does teaching a 'play to win' attitude in sport produce better athletes? Does this come at the expense of playing sport for fun?

▲ In 2005 Ofsted reported that well-managed sporting competition is being used to motivate pupils to try harder and raise standards.

FAIR PLAY

There are a number of issues relating to fair play that affect most sports around the world. The taking of banned substances that improve an athlete's performance is the main example of cheating, but fair play also relates to betting scandals and, less directly, the continued presence of racism in sport.

Punishing the cheats

The news that a high-profile athlete has tested positive for performance-enhancing drugs is always likely to be a big story, particularly during the Olympics. UK Sport attempts to encourage the highest standards of sporting conduct and leads an anti-drug programme. It is hoped that the efforts of UK Sport will continue to set a good example to British athletes up to and beyond the 2012 Olympics. UK Sport manages about 8000 drug tests a year in more than 50 sports. It has also launched the '100% Me' campaign. This is a platform for athletes to celebrate their successes as drug-free competitors.

It's a fix

Betting on the result of a game where the result has been influenced is known as 'match-fixing'. In 2006, leading football clubs

◄ British cyclist David Millar was found guilty of using the hormone EPO in 2004 and banned from competing for two years.

Clean Bowl Racism was launched by the ECB in 1999. Senior players carry the message that racism is not accepted in cricket. The Commission for Racial Equality has recently recognised the advances that cricket has made in tackling racism in the game.

◀ Cricket star Kevin Pietersen helps to launch an ECB initiative to encourage playing cricket in inner cities.

and referees in Italy were found guilty of colluding to fix matches in a scandal that shook Italian football to its foundations. While no football scandal in Britain has had the same impact, in 1999 a betting syndicate based in Asia attempted to sabotage floodlights at a Premiership ground to get the game abandoned at half-time, thereby allowing bets to stand on an unlikely half-time score. Investigations revealed that floodlights had been successfully tampered with at two other Premiership games. Betting scandals have also hit other sports, including cricket in South Africa, where players have been found to accept money from book-makers in order to 'throw', or lose a game, deliberately. In Britain, some jockeys have recently received bans for passing on inside information to book-makers or deliberately losing races.

Tackling racism

The government Department for Culture, Media and Sports supports the participation of those who have been under-represented in sport, for example athletes with disabilities and those from ethnic minorities. In the 1980s, many black players experienced hostility and racial abuse from football terraces, sometimes even from their own team's fans. The Kick Racism Out of Football group has led the campaign against racism in British football. Many football clubs now impose life bans on fans who abuse players. Britain's record now compares well with some other European countries, where racist chanting is still common amongst some supporters. The FA is also quick to respond to and act on reports of racism among players.

SPORT AND THE MEDIA

The popularity of sport in Britain is shown in the amount of attention that it receives in the press. Any success that British teams or sporting individuals achieve can make the newspaper front pages. However, sporting failures are also widely reported and this coverage can be very critical.

Hold the back page!

Sports writers are mainly keen to celebrate success in British sport. For example, many writers were delighted by the success of England's men and women's teams in the 2005 Ashes series. This was partly because they had reversed a losing record against the Australians that had continued for 18 years. But many writers were also pleased that, for once, another sport had 'knocked football off the back pages'.

Total football

Some people believe that there will come a point when there is too much football coverage. Andy Gray, the leading football commentator for Sky TV, admitted in a newspaper interview that he felt there were too many games on television. The concern is that with so many matches broadcast, the public will become bored of watching. There is also the concern that fewer fans are going to matches. As ticket prices continue to rise and more games are available to watch on satellite and digital television, overall attendances are dropping.

Fever pitch

The blanket coverage that football receives ignores the strong traditions that other sports have in Britain. While it is unlikely that these sports will die out, the achievements of all Britain's elite athletes need to be reported to inspire the next generation of competitors.

◀ Queen Elizabeth II held a reception to recognise the achievements of England's female cricketers in 2005.

Up for discussion

Even when they are successful, British teams have struggled to maintain their success. The recent achievements of the England rugby and cricket teams quickly gave way to a series of failures.

Typically, the reasons for this have received lots of media coverage. One of the reasons given is the failure of coaching staff to continue to motivate players to succeed. This argument goes that once players reach a peak, they need to be set new goals so that their competitive spirit is maintained.

Why do you think that recent British sporting success has so quickly turned to ashes?

Elevated expectations

It could be that the level of attention devoted to football and the other big sports raises expectations of success to unrealistic levels. It is possible that Britain is not much better or worse at sport than it was in 1966, when England won the football World Cup, or when Fred Perry became Wimbledon champion in 1936. It may just be that other nations have improved in the meantime, or perhaps their players do not have to compete under the same pressure to succeed.

▼ British sprinters celebrate winning gold in the men's 4 x 4 100 metre relay at the 2004 Olympic Games. British athletes have struggled to maintain success on the track and field since this famous victory.

SPORT AND NATIONAL PRIDE

One of the highest honours in sport is to represent one's country. The emotion on the faces of rugby players as they sing their national anthem before a game or the sight of a tearful Olympic champion standing on the podium as his or her national flag is raised shows how deeply patriotic pride is felt on the sporting field.

Pride and glory

Sport can be an important and acceptable way of showing national pride. This can be celebrated by following the fortunes of sportsmen and women representing a country. It is now common for the flag of St George to fly from cars in England during football tournaments. Fans can play an important part in motivating players by getting behind the team and cheering them on. A supportive crowd can be known as the 'twelfth man' of a team.

'Sing when you're winning'

The British attitude to sport can be an odd mix of arrogance and pessimism. Many believe that British competitors

▼ Welsh rugby fans show patriotic support with national team colours and songs.

should be the best in the world. This is perhaps because so many sports started in Britain. Pessimism is also a factor, maybe because expectations of our national sides are so high that they are easily disappointed.

Sporting success?

Meanwhile, Britain's actual sporting success is often underestimated. Athletes from Britain compete in a huge range of sports and there have been some notable victories in recent times. It may be unrealistic to expect Britain to perform any better in the 21st century. British-born sports have spread across the globe so successfully that many other nations are now represented by top athletes.

The old enemy

Countries that beat sports teams from Britain, particularly England, have always gained a special satisfaction from their success. This may be partly explained because the victory is seen as 'beating the team at its own game'. But there have been other issues at stake. The great West Indian cricketers of the 1980s delighted supporters by humbling teams from England, the country that had once governed the Caribbean islands.

'The English disease'

Patriotism can have an ugly face. British sport and its supporters have suffered from a bad reputation abroad due to the past behaviour of so-called football hooligans. Today, football hooliganism is partly controlled by sophisticated monitoring equipment, available to police and football authorities, that makes it difficult for known hooligans to attend matches. It has also been reduced by better policing, all-seater stadia and the widespread use of CCTV.

◀ Despite reaching three Grand Slam tennis tournament semi-finals, Tim Henman has yet to win any of tennis's major prizes.

CASE STUDY
'Bad luck, well played'

The British sporting public seems to admire and celebrate 'the plucky loser'. During Wimbledon, near-hysteria can greet British tennis stars, such as Tim Henman (right) on court, in spite of the fact that no British male player has progressed beyond the semi-finals since 1936, and no female player since 1977. It is unlikely that this would be the case in other countries, particularly the USA and Australia, where the attitude is 'first is first and second is nowhere'.

LOOKING TOWARDS 2012

▲ Children from East London stage a mini-Olympics in support of the 2012 bid.

In the past, Britain has enjoyed some spectacular sporting success. But rather than dwell on past glories, we must look forward to taking part in an increasingly competitive world environment. There is a great deal to be done before Britain is ready to host the 2012 Olympics, while social issues such as health and fitness and sporting participation levels also need to be explored and addressed.

Reasons for optimism

Outside of the most popular sports, young British sportsmen and women are competing at the highest levels. Plenty of young Olympic and Paralympic hopefuls are training hard to ensure that Great Britain achieves a level of success to match the faith that has been shown by UK Sport. Former Olympic gold medallist and chair of the 2012 Olympic bid, Lord Coe says, 'Britain performing well in 2012 is not the icing on the cake. It's pretty well the whole ingredient; it's crucial.'

The aim is to inspire more young British citizens to choose sport and follow in the footsteps of their Olympic heroes.

CASE STUDY
Emerging stars

- England cricketer Holly Colvin was named 2006 Female Pupil of the Year in the School Sport Matters national award winners. The campaign highlights excellence in school sport. During 2005, 15-year-old Colvin became the youngest player, male or female, to play Test cricket for England. She helped England reclaim the Ashes from Australia after 42 years. Holly received her award from a panel of sporting celebrities, including Olympic gold medallist Kelly Holmes, and Sports Minister Richard Caborn.

- The 20-year-old tennis player Andrew Murray is Scotland's brightest young sports star. Murray enjoyed a successful 2006, during which he beat the world's number one player, Roger Federer. He has received praise from some of the great tennis players, including Boris Becker, Martina Navratilova and John McEnroe. Wimbledon legend Bjorn Borg has tipped Murray to follow Federer as world number one. This talented young player has the ability, confidence and determination to become the most successful British tennis player for over 50 years.

- Welsh racing cyclist Nicole Cooke is 24 years old. In 2006, she became the world's number one female road cyclist. She was the winner of the 2006 *Grande Boucle*, the women's version of the Tour de France.

▼ Nicole Cooke crosses the finish line in the fifth stage of the *Grande Boucle* in June 2006.

GLOSSARY

Amateur Playing for no financial reward.

Arrogance Excessive confidence.

Banned substances Drugs that improve an athlete's performance or ability to train.

Betting tax Money that the government takes from people who gamble on the outcome of a game or race.

Book-makers People who arrange betting on the outcome of a game or race.

Commonwealth Games An international sports competition that takes place every four years. It involves teams from countries that have an association with the British commonwealth.

Conduct Behaviour.

Contract An agreement.

Elite Top level.

Facilities Sports stadia, training equipment and play areas.

Governing bodies Organisations that manage a particular area.

Grant An award of money.

Home nations England, Scotland, Wales and Northern Ireland.

Hooligans Fans who are involved in organising trouble and violent clashes.

Merchandising Clothing and other goods branded with a team's colours or emblem.

National Lottery Money raised by the sale of lottery tickets in Britain that is spent on sport, culture and other national causes.

Obesity Being overweight to an extent that is dangerous to a person's health.

Optimism Feeling positive or hopeful.

Participation Playing, as opposed to watching, sport.

Patriotic Showing pride in one's country.

Pessimism Feeling negative or without hope.

Premiership The top league in English football. Set up in 1992, it consists of 20 teams.

Professional Playing sport for money.

Recreation Taking part in an activity, such as sport, for fun.

Secretary of State A leading member of the British Government.

Spectator A person who goes to watch a an event.

Sponsorship A sum of money paid by a business to display its name or products.

Turnover The amount of business a company does in a set period of time.

FURTHER INFO

Books

How Sport is Organized by Kirk Bizley (Heinemann, 1997)
Issues in Sport Series Editor Craig Donnellan (Independence, 2003)
Sport in Society by Kirk Bizley (Heinemann, 1997)
Taking Part in Sport by Kirk Bizley (Heinemann, 1997)

Websites

www.uksport.gov.uk
The website for UK Sport

www.sportengland.org
The website for Sport England

www.sportni.net
The website for the Sports Council of
Northern Ireland

www.sports-council-wales.co.uk
The website for the Sports Council
of Wales

www.sportscotland.org.uk
The website for the Sports Council
of Scotland

**www.uksport.gov.uk/pages/
100_percent_me/**
The website for UK Sport's anti-drug
100% Me programme

www.london2012.com/en
The official website of the 2012 London
Olympic Games

www.sportingequals.com
The website for equal opportunities
in UK sport

www.kickitout.org
The website for anti-racism in football

www.paralympic.org
The official website of the International
Paralympic Committee

www.paralympics.org.uk
The official website of the British
Paralympic Association

http://news.bbc.co.uk/sport
The BBC sport website

**www.steveredgrave.com/charity/
index.htm**
The website of Steve Redgrave's
charitable trust

**Note to parents and teachers: Every effort
has been made by the Publishers to ensure
that these websites are suitable for children,
that they are of the highest educational
value, and that they contain no
inappropriate or offensive material.
However, because of the nature of the
Internet, it is impossible to guarantee that
the contents of these sites will not be
altered. We strongly advise that Internet
access is supervised by a responsible adult.**

INDEX

These are the lists of contents for each title in *British Issues:*

Future Energy

The importance of energy • The state of energy today • Declining fossil fuels • Climate change • The nuclear debate • Wind power • Water power • Power from the Sun • Power from the Earth • Energy from waste • Innovations • Saving energy • Government and citizen action

Population Change

Britain's changing faces • Measuring change • People in the past • Population at work • Changing families • New lifestyles • Life moves • Trading places • Immigrants and emigrants • The European Union • Cultural identity • Ageing population • Looking to the future

Sporting Success

2012 • A rich history • Governing bodies •Funding • Facilities • Sport and society • The business of sport • Success stories • Sport and education • Fair play • Sport and the media • Sport and national pride • Looking towards 2012

Sustainable Cities

What does it mean to be a sustainable city? • Urban versus rural populations • Planning sustainable cities • Urban regeneration • Issues in the south-east • Stuck in the city • City movers • Sustainable energy • Water • Dealing with waste • Urban wildlife • Cities of opportunity • Vision of the future

Waste and Recycling

What is waste? • Throwaway society • What happens to waste? • Why waste matters • Managing waste • Reduce and reuse • Recycle! • How recycling happens • Composting • Energy from waste • Why don't we recycle more? • Changing the rules • A way to go

Water

Desert Britain? • The water industry • Water supply • Household water • Industry and agriculture • A growing gap • Climate change • The cost of water • Saving water • Drinking water • Water and the environment • Planning for the future • New technology